Inventions That Shaped the World

NANCY ROBINSON MASTERS

Franklin Watts
A Division of Scholastic Inc.
New York • Toronto • London • Auckland • Sydney
Mexico City • New Delhi • Hong Kong
Danbury, Connecticut

Photographs © 2004: Brown Brothers: 14; Corbis Images: 16, 45, 55 (Bettmann), 8 (Christel Gerstenberg), 64 (Reuters NewMedia Inc.), 60 (Jim Richardson), 52 (Richard Hamilton Smith), cover bottom left, 10; Getty Images: 67 (AFP), cover top left, 65; Hulton|Archive/Getty Images: 32, 48; Library of Congress: 17 (via SODA), 6, 23, 39, 61; NASA: cover top left, 69; Peter Arnold Inc./Jim Olive: 51; Photo Researchers, NY/Alfred A. Hart Photo: 19; Smithsonian Institution, Washington, DC: 21; The Image Works: 68 (Francois Baille/Nice-Martin/Imapress), 57 (Francis de Richmond), chapter openers, 9, 12 (Science Museum, London/Topham-HIP), Time Life Pictures/Getty Images/Art Shay: 63; Wright State University, Special Collections and Archives: cover bottom right, 20, 22 right, 22 left, 25, 26, 36, 38, 41.

Cover design by Robert O'Brien and Kathleen Santini
Book production by Jeff Loppacker

Library of Congress Cataloging-in-Publication Data

Robinson Masters, Nancy.
The airplane / by Nancy Robinson Masters.
v. cm. — (Inventions that shaped the world)
Includes bibliographical references and index.
Contents: Twelve seconds that changed the world—Why fly?—The Wright men for the job—Inventing the flyer—The airplane and you—Flying into the future.

ISBN 0-531-12360-X (lib. bdg.) 0-531-16733-X (pbk.)

1. Aeronautics—History—Juvenile literature. 2. Airplanes—Juvenile literature 3. Aeronautics and civilization—Juvenile literature. [1. Aeronautics—History. 2. Airplanes.] I. Title. II. Series.
TL547.R567 2004
629.13'09—dc22 2003018930

1 2 3 4 5 6 7 8 9 10 R 13 12 11 10 09 08 07 06 05 04

Contents

CHAPTER ONE

Twelve Seconds That Changed the World

How long is twelve seconds? Take a deep breath. Twelve seconds is about the length of time you will be able to hold it before you have to take another breath. Walk fast. In twelve seconds you will take about sixty steps. Run hard. In twelve seconds you can travel about 120 feet (36 meters). That's not quite half the length of a football field.

On December 17, 1903, something happened for twelve seconds that people had dreamed of doing for thousands of years. It forever changed the world.

Powered by Flight

Johnny Moore was there when it took place. He was a sixteen-year-old boy who lived in Nags Head, North Carolina. Like other curious folks living on the ***Outer Banks*** of North

Carolina, Johnny often went to watch Wilbur and Orville Wright fly their ***gliders***. The Wright brothers were conducting experiments 4 miles (6.5 kilometers) from Kitty Hawk in the sand dunes beach area known as Kill Devil Hills.

Wilbur and Orville Wright spent three years testing their glider designs at Kitty Hawk before they flew their powered Flyer *on December 17, 1903.*

Johnny hoped this Thursday would be the day Wilbur and Orville tested their *Flyer.* The *Flyer* was not a glider. It had two wings, one above the other. There were two

propellers attached behind the wings. Unlike the gliders Johnny had seen them fly on other days, the *Flyer* had a gasoline-powered engine.

Johnny arrived at Kill Devil Hills in time to help John T. Daniels mount Orville's camera on a tall stand. Daniels had never taken a picture before. Three other men from the Coast Guard lifesaving station at Kitty Hawk had come to help the Wrights this icy-cold morning. Orville did not want to make the mistake other flying machine inventors had made. He wanted to be sure that he had a photograph. It would show the *Flyer* using power from its propellers worked by the small engine. Without a photograph he and Wilbur would have a hard time proving that they had done what the world's greatest scientists had not been able to do.

The Dream of Flying

Like most boys in 1903, Johnny had read McGuffey's *Readers* in school. A poem in the book, titled "Darius Green and His Flying Machine" by John Townsend Trowbridge, made fun of people who wanted to fly. Trowbridge wasn't the only person who was amused by such dreamers. Although in America and Europe there were often reports of men attempting to build ***heavier-than-air*** flying machines, newspaper editors considered these reports to be little more than fantasies.

FLYING AND GREEK MYTHOLOGY

Some people called Wilbur and Orville "the crazy buzzard boys." They compared the Wright brothers with characters in an ancient Greek myth. According to the myth, Daedalus and his son, Icarus, were prisoners on the Greek island of Crete. They fastened wings of feathers and beeswax to themselves to fly like birds and escape. Daedalus flew safely to Sicily, an island off the coast of Italy, but Icarus flew too near the sun. The wax on his wings melted, and he fell into the sea.

Would the wings on the Wright *Flyer* melt and fall into the Atlantic Ocean, Johnny wondered? He knew Wilbur and Orville would not be the first people to fly. A hot-air balloon had carried two men aloft in France in 1783. The men flew for twenty-five minutes and traveled 16 miles (26 km). However, they had no way to control the direction of the balloon.

Dirigibles were cigar-shaped balloons that could be steered. Johnny had a copy of the newspaper story telling how Count Ferdinand von Graf Zeppelin of Germany had flown a dirigible in 1900. The Wright brothers did not want to fly

This painting depicts the first flight of Count Ferdinand von Zeppelin's rigid airship, Zeppelin No. 1, *on July 2, 1900 over Lake Bodensee, Germany.*

a balloon or a dirigible. They wanted to fly a heavier-than-air machine with wings that could be controlled and would fly under its own power.

Wilbur and Orville ran a successful bicycle shop in their hometown of Dayton, Ohio. Johnny heard a man tell Daniels that the Wrights should stick with building bicycles. They were wasting their time building flying machines.

Inventors are not easily discouraged by what others say or think. Otto Lilienthal was this kind of inventor. The Wright brothers wanted to be like him. The German inventor made

German inventor Otto Lilienthal (1848-1896) began experimenting with gliders as a teenager. He became the world's leading aeronautical authority in the nineteenth century.

more than two thousand successful flights in his glider. He published *Bird Flight as the Basis for Aviation* in 1889. Wilbur and Orville carefully studied this book and all of Lilienthal's research.

Lilienthal died in a glider crash in 1896 just as he was preparing to attempt powered flight. Wilbur and Orville determined to continue his efforts to invent a powered, heavier-than-air flying machine. They also studied the work of the inventor Octave Chanute. They built the *Flyer* using many of Chanute's designs.

Into the North Wind

It took three years of hard work and many experiments before they could build the *Flyer*. A lot of the experiments were simple, others were difficult, and some ended in disaster. Just three days earlier, Wilbur crashed on takeoff. He had won the flip of the coin to be the first to fly. Now it was Orville's turn.

At 10:35 A.M. on December 17, 1903, the *Flyer* was repaired and ready for flight. Orville's camera was also ready. It was his turn to be the pilot. Wilbur checked the north winds blowing at Kitty Hawk one more time. That morning the wind had been as high as 30 miles (48 km) per hour. Should they go ahead? Wilbur asked. Orville nodded yes.

Johnny watched as Orville carefully laid on his stomach on the lower wing of the *Flyer*. He grasped the controls to steer the twin ***rudders***. The 12-horsepower engine fired. The propellers turned. The *Flyer* began moving down the

This model shows the Wright Flyer *sliding down the launch rail at Kitty Hawk with Orville as the pilot and Wilbur running alongside to steady the wing.*

launch track into the north wind. Wilbur ran alongside, holding the right wing to keep the flyer balanced. Suddenly, the machine rose 10 feet (3 m) above the sands of Kill Devil Hills. Orville worked the controls to keep the wobbly *Flyer* going as straight and level as he could.

John T. Daniels waited no longer. He photographed the *Flyer* just as it rose into the air. Twelve seconds after lifting off, Orville and the *Flyer* landed with a thud on the soft sand. They had flown 120 feet (41 m). It was the first controlled flight of a powered, heavier-than-air vehicle with a pilot onboard. They had a photograph to prove it!

CHAPTER TWO

Why Fly?

The desire to fly is an idea handed down to us by our ancestors. . . . [They] looked enviously on the birds soaring freely through space, above all obstacles, on the infinite highway of the air.

—Wilbur Wright,* The Patriot *Archives, 1911

For Wilbur and Orville Wright, the desire to soar like the birds was reason enough to fly. They were also intrigued by the challenge of doing something others had never done. However, there were other reasons that were shared by many people who wanted to fly.

To Take to the Sky

Curiosity was the first reason people wanted to fly. They wanted a way to go places they had never been and to see things they had never seen. People were also curious about other people. ***Isolation*** was a common lifestyle prior to the invention of the airplane. There were, and still are, remote areas of the world where there are no roads, and where railroads and ships cannot go.

The second reason people wanted to fly was for improved protection. For centuries, people had built towers on castles and on bridges to be able to see an enemy army approaching. Early experiments with ***lighter-than-air*** balloons had

A basket carrying observers was attached to a balloon filled with hot air and flown near battlefields to view enemy activity during the American Civil War.

proved that the ability to see a battlefield from the air in warfare was a tremendous advantage.

Military leaders wanted to be in control of the air just as they wanted to be in control of the land and oceans. This was especially true in the United States as it expanded across the continent.

TRADING WITH CHINA

In 1275, Venetian explorer Marco Polo hoped to find a trade route to China. His trip took almost five years to complete. Today, the distance Marco Polo traveled can be covered in a jet airplane in about five hours.

By far the most important reason people wanted to fly was the need to travel faster. Unless you were a very wealthy person who did not have to work, you did not have the time to travel great distances. The time required to transport goods by wagon or ship often made it impossible to trade ***perishable*** items.

People needed faster methods to communicate. In 1860 the Pony Express riders' relay on horseback took up to ten days to carry mail from Missouri to California. Money sometimes did not reach a bank in time for a merchant to be able to purchase supplies. Medicine failed to arrive in time to treat a sick child. A letter from a gentleman

Galloping horses carried Pony Express riders like the young man in this painting. This was the fastest method for transporting mail across America in 1860.

proposing marriage often arrived after the intended bride had wed someone else!

Walking was the earliest form of transportation. Depending on the terrain and physical condition of a person, he or she could walk several miles an hour. However, someone pushing a wheelbarrow filled with bricks or grain had to travel much slower.

THE NEED FOR SPEED

A great ***migration*** of people arrived in America in the eighteenth and nineteenth centuries. They spent six to fourteen weeks living in crowded, unsanitary conditions aboard ships. Lengthy exposure to disease and malnutrition on the ships resulted in death for thousands of immigrants before and after they reached America. Immigrants who fly to America can now make this trip in less than a day.

Starvation could occur due to the inability of people to move quickly enough into areas where food was available. American Indians dug canals and built canoes in order to expand their fishing and hunting territories. A hunter might have to paddle all day to find adequate food.

Slow ships carrying cargo were easy prey for pirates. Not only was cargo stolen, but sailors were kidnapped to serve as crew members on pirate vessels. Freighters leaving the East Coast of the United States spent several months sailing around the tip of South America to get to the West Coast. The amount of time the ships were exposed to the threat of piracy was a constant concern.

Practical Progress

Completed in 1869, the ***transcontinental*** railroad provided some solutions for dealing with the transportation challenges of time and distance. Traveling at an average of 25 miles (40 km) per hour, trains could deliver freight and passengers five times faster than a boat on a canal could. However, a canal could go only where it had been dug. Trains could go only where tracks had been laid. The sky did not have these limitations.

A nineteenth-century English visionary, Sir George Cayley, predicted the solution to these obstacles almost a hundred years before the Wright brothers' success at Kitty Hawk. He stated, "I am well convinced that aerial

Hundreds of immigrant laborers worked under dangerous conditions to build the tracks for the Central Pacific Railroad.

navigation will form a most prominent feature in the progress of civilization."

In 1903 an automobile was driven from San Francisco, California, to New York in only sixty-three days. This was an amazing accomplishment when compared with a horse-drawn wagon, which traveled at a top speed of 15 miles (24 km)

Orville Wright (driving), Katharine Wright, and Harriet Stillman go for a ride in an automobile built by the Motor Carriage Company in 1903.

a day. However, there were fewer than 150 miles (241 km) of paved roads in the United States, and the practical use of the automobile was not yet apparent.

The "infinite highway of the air" appealed to the Wright brothers and other inventors. It also appealed to the curious, the cautious, and the time-conscious citizen. Many wanted to fly, but unlike birds, they did not have wings to soar.

CHAPTER THREE

The Wright Men for the Job

The heroes that Johnny Moore had read about in books didn't look like the ordinary men making the very first powered, heavier-than-air flight right before his eyes that December 17, 1903. Wilbur Wright was tall and thin with bright blue eyes. He did not wear a beard or mustache and was already bald. Johnny had almost never seen Wilbur not wearing a hat or cap.

Orville (left) and Wilbur Wright (right) credited their successes as inventors to their mutual respect for each other's ideas and skills.

MILTON AND SUSAN WRIGHT

Milton Wright (1829–1917) was a bishop in the Church of the United Brethren in Christ. When he returned from travels, he often brought souvenirs to the children. One souvenir was a toy helicopter-like top powered by a rubber band. It was based on a design for a flying machine by scientist Alphonse Penaud. Bishop Wright did not know the toy would spark the passion for flying that Wilbur and Orville later shared.

Susan Wright (1831–1889) was a most unusual girl for the time in which she grew up. She liked helping her father in his workshop. She learned how to draw plans and use tools to build sleds and horse-drawn carriages.

Susan attended Hartville College in Indiana. Her grades in math were the best of all the students. After marrying Milton Wright, she enjoyed teaching mechanical skills to her children.

Orville Wright was a bit shorter and heavier than Wilbur. He had a mustache and the same bright blue eyes as his brother. Both men were extremely shy with people.

This photograph of Wilbur Wright was taken about 1871.

Young Wilbur Wright

Wilbur was born on April 16, 1867, on a farm near Millville, Indiana. He was the third child of Milton and Susan Catherine Wright. The family moved to Dayton, Ohio when Wilbur was two years old.

Wilbur's two older brothers, Reuchlin (pronounced Rooshlin) and Lorin, helped take care of Wilbur. When Wilbur was four years old, Orville was born.

The Wright family moved from Dayton to Richmond, Indiana, where Wilbur attended high school. Like his mother, he was an excellent student. Like his father, he believed in discipline, which helped him become an outstanding athlete.

The Wright family moved back to Dayton just before Wilbur was to graduate. He made good grades, but did not apply for a diploma in Richmond. He attended Central High School in Dayton the following year to study trigonometry.

Stopped in His Skates

Milton and Susan planned for Wilbur to attend Yale University. When Wilbur was seventeen, an ice-skating accident changed those plans. He and several other young men were playing ice hockey. A hockey stick accidentally flew out of the hand of another skater and hit Wilbur in the face. The injury did not seem serious at the time, but a few weeks later he began having what was diagnosed as "a nervous heart." That ended his formal education.

THE WRIGHT PARTNERSHIP

The first time the two boys referred to themselves as "the Wright brothers" was when they started their printing business. They built their first printing press from a damaged tombstone and used buggy parts. The newspaper they started failed, but they continued to be partners in the print shop.

Young Orville Wright

Orville Wright was born on August 19, 1871, at the Wright home at 7 Hawthorne Street in Dayton, Ohio. The large

Ten-year-old Orville Wright was four years younger than Wilbur. According to Wilbur, "we lived together, played together, worked together and, in fact, thought together."

two-story home was usually cluttered with parts and pieces of items Susan and the children were curious about. They spent many happy hours taking things apart to see what made them work and putting them back together again.

THE WRIGHT SISTER

Katharine Wright (1874–1929) was the youngest of the Wright children. She was the only child to complete college. She earned a teaching certificate from Oberlin College in 1898.

In 1908 Katharine helped demonstrate the airplane by flying with Wilbur in France. Her signature appears on the shares of stock sold by the Wright Airplane Manufacturing Company.

Exactly three years later, on August 19, 1874, Katharine Wright was born. The Wright children were not given middle names, but each had a nickname. Wilbur was "Ullam." Orville was "Bubs." Katharine was "Swes," which means "little sister" in German. Will, Orv, and Kate were very close while growing up.

The three made a promise to each other never to marry. Wilbur and Orville kept their promise. Katharine did not. She married Henry Haskell in 1926.

A Curious Education

Orville did well in elementary school. He did not do well in high school except in science classes. Watching buzzards fly, building sleds, and drawing pictures of his ideas for new inventions interested him more than studying required subjects. "We were lucky enough to grow up in an environment where there was always much encouragement to investigate whatever aroused curiosity," Orville said.

Neither Orville nor Wilbur received high school diplomas. They were later awarded a total of fifteen honorary degrees from colleges and universities in the United States and Europe.

Bicycle Business for Two

In 1892 the brothers formed a business building bicycles. By 1899, however, they were spending more time watching birds fly than building bicycles. Wilbur wrote a letter to scientist Octave Chanute. Chanute had been gathering and organizing information about flight. "For some years I have been afflicted with the belief that flight is possible to man," Wilbur wrote.

As the world prepared to move into a new century, the Wright brothers prepared to move into a new career. They knew this daring venture would change their lives. However, they did not know that it would change the world.

CHAPTER FOUR

Inventing the Flyer

"They did it! They did it!"
—Johnny Moore

Johnny Moore ran into Kitty Hawk on the afternoon of December 17, 1903, with the news. The *Flyer* built by the Wright brothers had made four successful flights that morning!

How did Wilbur and Orville Wright do what no one else had been able to? There are several answers to this question. The first can be found in a letter Wilbur wrote to the Smithsonian Institution in Washington, D.C., more than four years before their success at Kitty Hawk: "I believe that simple flight is possible to man," Wilbur wrote. "The experiments and investigations will result in the accumulation of information and knowledge and skill which will finally lead to accomplished flight."

Experiments.

Investigations.

Information.

Knowledge.

Skill.

In just one sentence, Wilbur named the most important tools used by inventors. He and Orville used each of these tools throughout all their efforts to build a heavier-than-air flying machine that could be powered and controlled in sustained flight. Without any one of these tools, it is highly unlikely they would have succeeded.

Early Birds

One reason the Wrights succeeded was that they adopted their research methods from engineer and inventor Octave Chanute. Like Chanute, they concentrated on developing solutions to problems by using a step-by-step approach. First, they assembled and described all known information and data. Next, they listed all the known problems. Then, they discussed and documented every possible solution to the problem.

While they worked in their bicycle shop, they read Chanute's book, *Progress in Flying Machines*, out loud to each other. The book, published in 1894, was filled with

MAIN PARTS OF AN AIRPLANE

Wings: Wings provide lift and support the weight of the aircraft and its contents while in flight.

Propeller: A propeller is a rotating blade attached to the front or rear of an engine that moves in a vertical circle to push air over and under the wings.

Rudder: The rudder is the movable vertical section of the tail that controls side-to-side movement.

Horizontal stabilizer: The horizontal stabilizer is the horizontal surface section of the tail used to balance the airplane.

Elevator: The elevator is the movable horizontal section of the tail that causes the plane to move up and down.

Ailerons: Ailerons are outward movable sections of an airplane's wings that move in opposite directions (one up, one down). They are used to make coordinated turns.

Fuselage: The central body section of an airplane.

diagrams of the earliest efforts to construct flying machines. It brought together in one volume the history of man's attempts to fly. For example, the book included information about Italian genius Leonardo da Vinci's ornithopter.

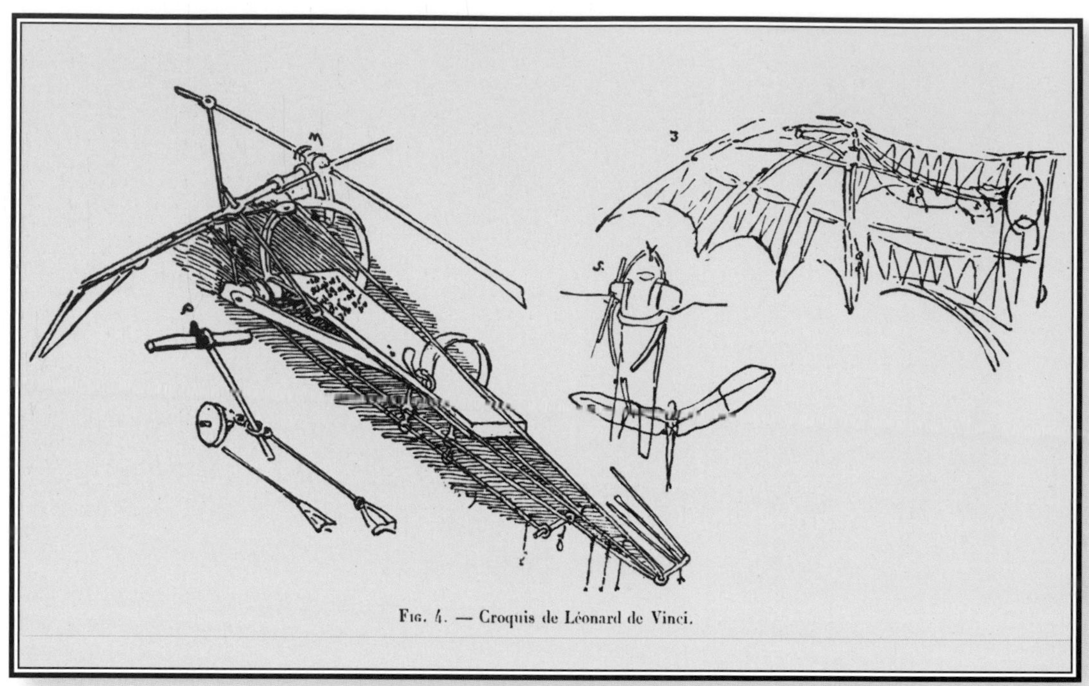

Today's modern helicopter closely resembles sketches of an ornithopter drawn by Italian artist Leonardo da Vinci about 1485.

The ornithopter, with its whirling wings, was one of more than one hundred drawings made by da Vinci in the 1480s. It was never built, but his concept of a whirling wing is seen in today's helicopter.

Chanute's book also contained drawings of inventions that looked like birds. Several early inventors met their deaths trying to flap gigantic wings with their arms as they leaped from barns and cliffs. While it is easy to laugh at these efforts today, it must be remembered that there was no technology at the time to provide a better way to achieve flight than to imitate birds.

FORCE FACTORS

The four forces that act on an airplane are lift, weight, thrust, and drag.

- Lift comes from air moving over the wings. The air under the wings pushes up more than the air on top of the wings pushes down.
- Weight is caused by gravity. Weight pulls downward on the airplane.
- Thrust, caused by an airplane's engine, pushes the airplane forward.
- Drag tries to slow down a moving object. Drag is the force that opposes thrust.

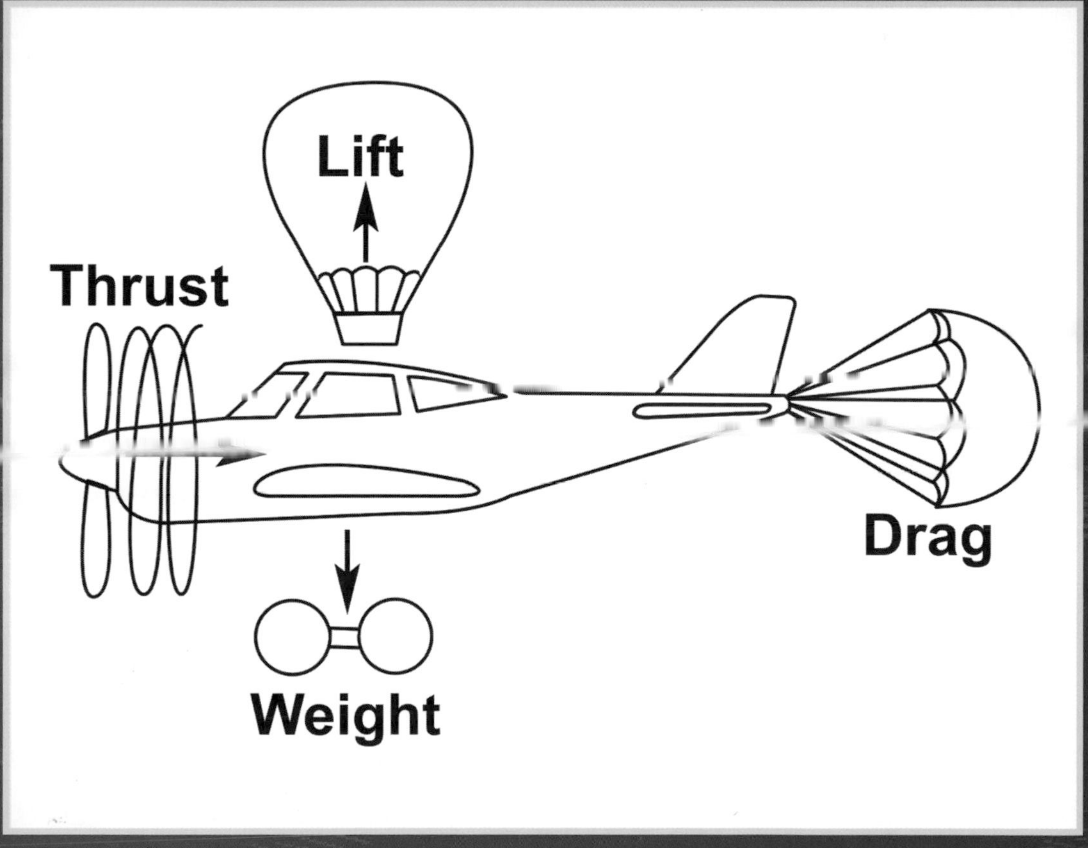

It took three years of gathering information, investigating the experiments of others, and analyzing this data for the Wrights to agree they had to solve three main problems. First, they had to invent a method for controlling the machine in flight. Second, they had to design wings that would provide sufficient lift to carry the weight of the machine, an engine, and a person. Third, they had to build an engine to produce sufficient power to sustain the flight through the air.

The Wright brothers were about to develop a method for inventing that was radically different from the one used by other inventors of their time. Their method was to solve each problem independently of the other problems. They would use the solution to each problem to fit the pieces together to produce a controllable, heavier-than-air machine that could sustain flight.

Inventing a Method of Control

One day a customer came into the cycle shop to purchase a new bicycle inner tube. While they were talking, Wilbur absentmindedly twisted each end of the inner tube's cardboard box in opposite directions.

That was it! The solution to the problem of how to control a rigid wing while it was in flight was right there in his hands. Wilbur realized that instead of moving the entire wing for lateral control as so many other inventors had done, they only needed to twist the tips of the wings. When Wilbur told Orville what he had discovered, Orville realized this was exactly what he had observed while watching buzzards. They did not flap their entire wings, but raised and lowered the wing tips to control their flight.

The Wrights constructed a kite that had a pair of wings 5 feet (1.5 m) long and 13 inches (33 centimeters) wide with a horizontal tail. On the end of each of the kite's wingtips they attached long cords.

Wilbur took the kite to a field near Dayton and launched it. He was able to control the kite's lateral movements while standing on the ground, pulling the cords attached to the wingtips. This "wing-warping" experiment was a success! Later the Wrights designed a system of wires and pulleys between the wingtips and the hammocklike section of the wing where the pilot would lie. When the pilot laid on the lower wing, his hips were positioned inside a hip cradle. The hip cradle was fastened to a slot

MOTION MATTERS

Motions that must be controlled in order to fly are pitch, yaw, and roll.

- Pitch is the up and down movement of an airplane.
- Yaw is the side-to-side movement of an airplane.
- Roll is turning along the length of an airplane.

Orville and Wilbur Wright were the first to test the concept of warping the wings of an airplane. The warping is visible in the twisted shape of the upper and lower wings.

that let it slide from side to side like a swinging hammock. The hip cradle activated the wing-warping mechanism. The wing-warping mechanism was a series of wires and pulleys attached to the outer edges of the wings that turned the back edge of one wing up and the other down at the same time. So by swaying his hips in the wing hammock, the pilot could twist the wingtips up or down. This gave the pilot the ability to make a controlled turn. The wing-warping discovery is considered by many to be the most important contribution the Wrights made to flight technology.

Calculating Lift

The Wrights were among the first to realize that a flying machine could not be built that imitated birds. However, they agreed that inventor Otto Lilienthal's experiments had proved beyond a shadow of a doubt that flight in a heavier-than-air machine was possible. His experiments had produced a table of formulas all inventors were using to determine the amount of lift produced by different sizes and shapes of **airfoils** (curved wings). Unfortunately, Lilienthal's lift tables contained some incorrect information.

It is important to remember that none of these inventors had the benefit of an electronic calculator or computer program to use. Each math problem had to be solved using pencil, paper, and algebra, geometry, or trigonometry skills.

If you had stepped into the tent erected by the Wright brothers on the sands of Kill Devil Hills during their glider tests in 1900 and 1901, you would have felt their frustration and disappointment. The gliders they had built using Lilienthal's lift tables did not perform as they had expected. They returned to Dayton after these discouraging experiments and spent each evening at the Wright home discussing the mysterious lack of lift. The more they talked, the more they asked each other the same question: Could Lilienthal's formulas be wrong?

To find the answer, the Wrights conducted an experiment by riding around Dayton with a horizontal wheel mounted on the handlebars of a bicycle. On this horizontal wheel they attached two airfoils at right angles to each other—one curved and one flat. If the tables were correct, the pressure of the two airfoils would balance each other out, and the wheel would not move.

The wheel moved! Now they were sure the Lilienthal formulas they had used to calculate the exact size and shape for their glider wings were wrong.

They decided to build a wind tunnel to be used in creating new formulas. The Wrights did not invent the concept of the wind tunnel; they were, however, the first inventors to use one to conduct extensive experiments with multiple wing

This is a replica of the original Wright wind tunnel constructed by Orville and Wilbur to compute the correct lift data necessary to build the Flyer's *wings.*

surfaces. The wind tunnel they built was a pine box 16 inches (40.5 cm) square and 6 feet (1.8 m) long with a window of glass in the top. A measuring device called "the balance" was made from an old hacksaw blade and bicycle-spoke wire. A one-cylinder gasoline engine powered the fan that pushed air through the wind tunnel in which models of wings were suspended at different angles. A gauge inside the box tested the effects of air pressure on nearly two hundred shapes and sizes of wings. From these experiments the Wrights calculated new formulas to determine the correct shape and size of a wing to have adequate lift for a specific weight.

In 1902 the brothers returned to Kitty Hawk with a glider they had built using their wind tunnel formulas. It flew exactly

Wilbur Wright and Dan Tate test fly a glider at Kitty Hawk in 1902. Tate was one of several men from the local area who helped the Wrights conduct their experiments.

as they had predicted. However, adjustments now had to be made to other parts of the glider, including repositioning the tail. This became a constant part of the invention process—changing the size, shape, or location of one part called for changing the size, shape, and location of other parts.

"As famous as we became for our *Flyer* and its system of control, it all would never have happened if we had not developed our own wind tunnel and derived our own correct data," Wilbur later wrote.

HOW A GASOLINE ENGINE WORKS

- The engine mixes fuel with oxygen in a combustion (pressure) chamber.
- The mixture is ignited by a spark.
- The burning mixture creates hot, expanding gases.
- The gases push a ***piston***. As the piston moves, it produces power.

Inventing a Power Plant

Wilbur and Orville turned their attention to the problem of sustaining flight. They needed a lightweight engine to provide the thrust required to overcome drag. They also had to have propellers that could transform the power of the engine into forward thrust. This combination of engine and propellers would be the *Flyer*'s power plant.

Orville used a pencil to sketch the design for the first Wright engine on a piece of brown wrapping paper. Mechanic Charlie Taylor, who worked in the Wright Cycle Company, then built the engine mostly from bicycle parts. Taylor would later build every engine for all the airplanes the Wrights produced.

Wilbur and Orville didn't think designing the propellers for the engine would take very long. They were wrong. According to Wilbur, the problem of designing the propellers "became more complex the longer we studied it. With the machine

A curious, but cautious, U.S. military cavalryman studies the radiator, engine, and chain drive of the Wright Model "A" Flyer.

moving forward, the air flying backward, the propellers turning sidewise, and nothing standing still, it seemed impossible to find a starting point from which to trace the various reactions."

It took them three months of poring over hundreds of measurements and calculations to produce the pair of 8.5-foot (2.6-m) carved wooden propellers. These propellers, made of spruce, had been shaped by the Wrights with hand-held hatchets and knives. They were mounted at the rear of the wings as pushers spinning in opposite directions. The propellers were so precisely built using the Wright brothers' formulas that they produced 99 percent of the thrust they were designed to provide.

The Wrights argued loud and often while inventing the engine and propellers. Tension in the workshop ran high. Each constantly checked the other's work for mistakes. How did they remain partners in this atmosphere?

Orville Wright laid on his stomach in a hammocklike section of the lower wing when he made the first successful powered, controlled flight of a heavier-than-air flying machine. The hammock was attached to the tips of the wings of the flyer by a system of wires and pulleys. By shifting his weight from side to side as he lay in the wing hammock, Orville was able to move the tips of the wings up or down. This "wing-warping" technique made it possible to control the direction of the airplane in the air. Orville and Wilbur Wright were the first inventors to discover this method of controlling the airplane.

"After we argued, we always worked out a new theory," Orville explained.

It took the Wrights more than four years to invent the solutions for control, lift, and power for flight. The result was one invention made up of many parts. The *Flyer* the Wrights assembled in December 1903 had a framework of spruce and ash wood covered in cotton cloth. It measured 21 feet 1 inch (6.5 m) long, 9 feet 4 inches (2.8 m) high, with a wingspan of 40 feet 4 inches (12.3 m). Including the engine and propellers, the machine weighed 605 pounds (272 kg). Add the weight of Orville Wright, and the result was the 750-pound (338-kg) combination of man and machine that Johnny Moore saw lift off the ground and fly in controlled, sustained, powered flight above the sands of Kitty Hawk.

It truly was the Wright *Flyer*.

Patent Problems

The Wrights filed for a ***patent*** based on their 1902 glider design on March 23, 1903. A patent is a claim of ownership of an invention. Other inventors soon claimed ownership of flying machine designs.

By 1905 the Wrights were so busy defending their claims of ownership related to the *Flyer* that they stopped working on improvements to it. They later resumed inventing, but they became much more secretive about their work. On

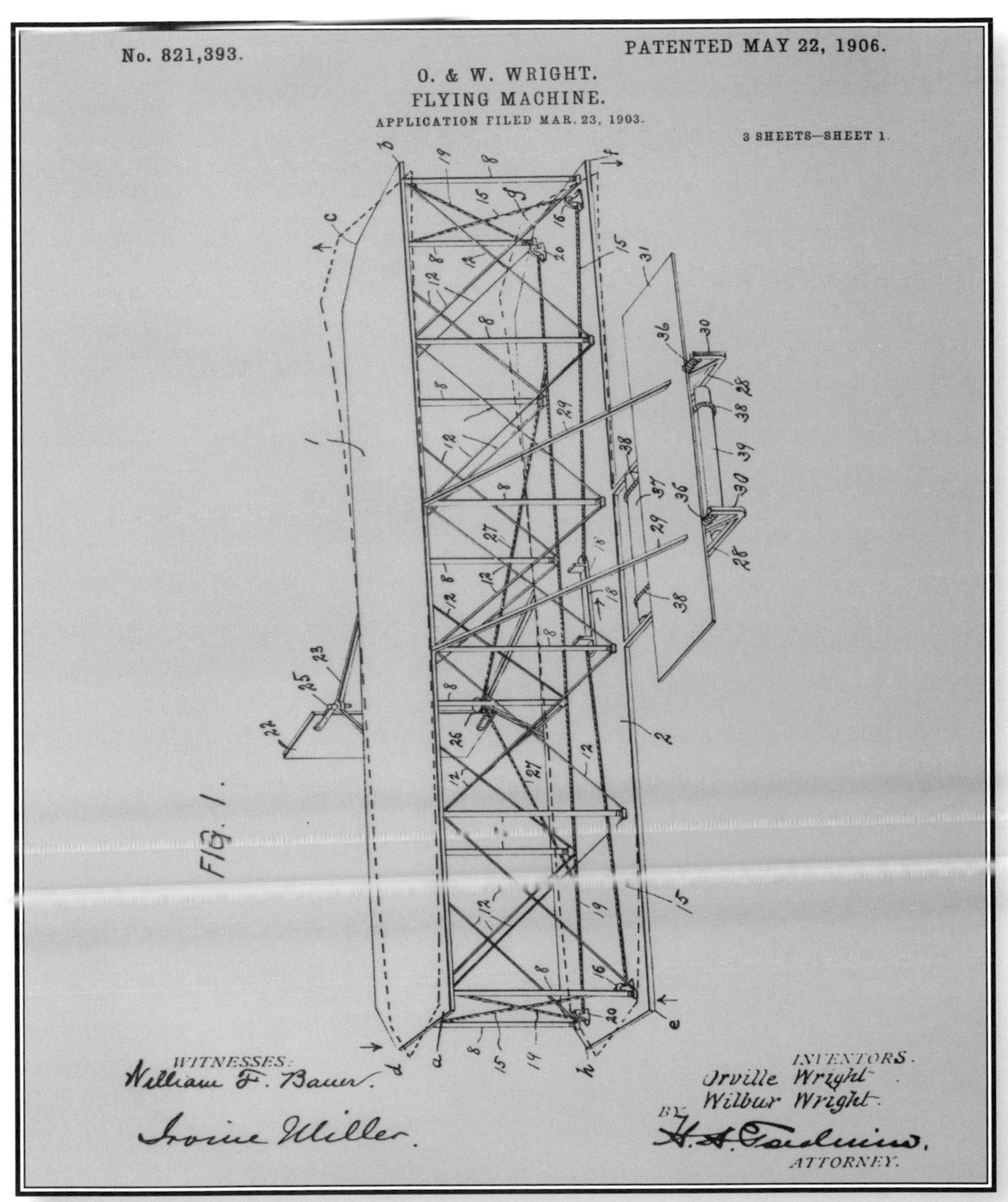

This patent issued May 22, 1906, granted the Wright brothers "the exclusive right to make, use and vend the said invention" for the next seventeen years.

May 22, 1906, the U.S. government finally issued the Wright brothers the first patent on their flying machine.

The Wrights were able to prove their claims of ownership to most of their inventions with the photographs they wisely took while they were conducting their experiments. Each photograph was carefully identified by date, time, and location. The hundreds of pages of notes the Wrights had recorded in their journals about their experiments also provided evidence for their claims of ownership.

Patent problems continued for several years. Eventually these problems were resolved, although arguments continue to this day as to who actually invented some of the designs used by the Wrights.

Wilbur Wright died of typhoid fever in 1912, but Orville lived until 1948, when he died from a heart attack.

CHAPTER FIVE

The Airplane and You

The airplane has touched the lives of almost everybody living today. At first only a few people believed the claims the Wright brothers made about their invention. Their story of what happened at Kitty Hawk was received much as stories of flying saucers are received today. Gradually people began to understand that the flight of the Wright *Flyer* was one of the greatest achievements of modern civilization.

You may never have ridden in an airplane or been to an airport. Even if the only airplanes you have ever seen are those shown on television or in movies, the airplane is an invention that has become a vital part of your daily life. Let's look at some of the ways airplanes have made an impact on our world and on each of us.

The Way We Live

The airplane changed how we viewed the world around us. Before World War I (1914–1918) "air meets" brought together huge crowds of people from different social backgrounds. The earliest attempts to fly were inspired by a simple desire to solve the problem of mechanical flight.

By 1909, crowds were flocking to air meets in Europe as well as America where builders hoped to attract buyers for their flying machines.

The prospect of winning prizes of silver cups or cash in aerial competitions, however, soon created an explosion of new aviation technology. The race was on for inventors to build faster, more reliable flying machines.

In 1910 more than seventy different types of engines were being constructed for air meet competitions in the United States and Europe. According to Igor Sikorsky, one of the world's greatest aeronautical engineers, "Most of the airplane design knowledge used in World War I was discovered by an inventor willing to risk his reputation or his life before a crowd of curious air meet spectators."

Air meets and air races were primarily funded by wealthy investors and newspapers seeking to build readerships. In 1911 more than a million dollars in air meet competition prize money was awarded. One pilot collected an enormous sum of money when he made the first night flight over Paris, France. His ***biplane*** was outfitted with electric lightbulbs.

Early air meets not only attracted machines capable of intense sport competition, but also led to the production of airplanes capable of aerial combat. Some saw this as a step toward greater military security; others thought this was a step backward for society. All agreed that the airplane had made the world smaller. Nations once separated by time and distance had become neighbors. The airplane united some of these neighbors and divided others.

THE LANGUAGE OF FLIGHT

Because airplanes can cover great distances in short periods of time, a common language needs to be spoken by pilots. International law designates English as the language all pilots and air traffic controllers are required to use during flight operations.

For example, all communications broadcast by a pilot flying an airplane that takes off in Rome, Italy, and lands in Berlin, Germany, must be spoken in English. Without a common language, the chances of confusion in communications would be enormous. It would make safe flight impossible.

Carrying mail by airplane had proved successful in demonstration flights before World War I. The war confirmed that the airplane could be developed as a reliable means of fast commercial and mail transportation. On May 15, 1918, the U.S. Congress officially established airmail service between New York City and Washington, D.C. Within three years the Post Office Department adopted the DeHavilland plane with a Liberty twelve-cylinder engine as their standard equipment. These mail planes were considered speedy and capable of carrying a mail load of 500 pounds (187 kg).

The demand for more airmail routes and bigger and better planes grew quickly. This, in turn, required more airports and more maintenance facilities along the routes. By the time of

A Boeing 757 jet aircraft can be equipped with pallets instead of passenger seats for transporting enormous loads of cargo to locations around the world.

the first transpacific airmail flight in 1935, thousands of people were employed in this industry.

Carrying mail and moving freight by air has dramatically changed our lifestyles. Many routes established by early airmail pilots are the ***airways*** used today by companies operating global cargo services. We can receive a letter or a machinery part needed to keep our refrigerators, automobiles, and computers operating in just a matter of hours instead of days.

Airplanes can carry medicine, blood, and tissue to patients awaiting organ transplants. The airplane has made it possible to save lives by saving time.

Airplanes used for agriculture are making some of the most important changes in the way we meet the increasing demand to produce food to feed the world. Airplanes are used to plant and fertilize crops, and to reduce disease

CROP DUSTERS AND AIR TRACTORS

Older methods of applying chemicals to crops used chemicals in powder form. Pilots who flew airplanes to apply this powder became known as "crop dusters," as did their planes.

Now airplanes apply chemicals in liquid form. These "air tractors," equipped with computer technology, can tailor the spray of environmentally safe chemicals to the exact size of a field.

and populations of destructive insects. For example, all rice fields in the United States are planted by airplanes.

Airplanes are also designed and built specifically for battling forest fires and to aid in reforesting areas that have been destroyed by fire or disease. Feeding livestock and redistributing wildlife to improve food supplies for animals in developing nations has helped people become more productive with their own natural resources. Aerial photography is used for finding and mapping water supplies. We even use airplanes to change the weather through cloud seeding to produce rain.

HOW AIRPLANES ARE USED TO MAKE IT RAIN

Cloud seeding is part of the science known as weather modification. The pilot flies the airplane into selected clouds. The clouds must contain water droplets at below-freezing temperatures. Flares attached to the airplane shoot yellow powder particles of silver iodide into the clouds. When the particles of silver iodide meet the cold-water droplets, they trigger the formation of ice crystals and raindrops. Some cloud-seeding flights are successful, though others are not.

The Ways We Work

In the early 1920s pilots known as barnstormers took the airplane to the people by traveling from town to town, giving rides and performing aerial displays and stunts. Barnstormers got their name from flying through barns to demonstrate their skills as pilots. They created a desire to fly among the public, which led to the growing demand for passenger service.

In 1926 the U.S. government recognized the impact the airplane was having on the nation's economy. The Air Commerce Act became law. It gave the federal government the responsibility of regulating the use of airspace to best suit the needs of the people and the nation.

Airplanes changed the way we did business. Moving people and products by air allowed businesspeople to meet with customers without spending many days traveling. Buses and trains suffered losses because airplanes could move people faster. However, because people could travel faster, more people began to travel. This produced the need for more travel-related services, such as hotels, motels, restaurants, and taxis.

Women in the Workforce

World War II saw thousands of women who had never worked outside their homes taking jobs in factories and businesses to replace the men who had gone to perform military service. When the war ended, many women chose to remain in the public workforce. Women who worked as stewardesses (flight attendants) helped commercial air travel become accepted as a safe and desirable method of

Women at the Philadelphia Naval Aircraft Factory assemble a wing for an airplane soon to be flown in combat in World War II.

transportation for families as well as for businesspeople. Today, men as well as women work as flight attendants.

Smaller towns and cities were bypassed by commercial airlines that could not afford to operate large aircraft to carry small numbers of passengers. This resulted in the growth of a new segment of aviation called general aviation. All aircraft that are not commercial airliners or military aircraft are general aviation aircraft. There are more than ten thousand aircraft serving general aviation airlines around the world. General aviation planes carry passengers as well as cargo.

Just as the airplane affected the economy, the economy affected the airplane. Competition to make air travel affordable for all people resulted in a new law in 1978. The Airline Deregulation Act allowed airlines to choose their routes and rates. Airfares decreased, so more people could afford to fly.

PASSENGERS AND PROGRESS

In 1975 the number of people who flew on U.S. airlines was 205 million. Five years later that number soared to 297 million people. In 2000 U.S. airlines carried 666 million passengers.

The Wright brothers employed fewer than a dozen people in their aircraft-building business. By 1980 more than 350,000 people worked for airlines all over the world. In 2000 there were more than 730,000 people employed in the air industry. This was more people than were employed in automobile manufacturing that same year.

The Way We Play

Not everyone traveling by air does so for business reasons. Many travel for pleasure. Airfares between New York and Los Angeles aboard a commercial airliner sometimes cost less than driving a car that distance would.

To encourage passengers to fly commercially, new aircraft competitions were sponsored. In 1931 James H. (Jimmy) Doolittle won the first Bendix Trophy transcontinental race.

The next ten years became known as "the Golden Age" of airplane development. Speed, distance, and altitude records were sometimes set and broken within the same week. Doolittle's later race in the "Gee Bee" airplane, with its short wings and high-powered engine, revolutionized the thinking of aircraft designers. The sponsor of an aviation "first" usually gained the admiration of the public, and this increased the demand for their products and services.

Today, flight attendants are no longer required to be unmarried, registered nurses as was the requirement in the early days of airline passenger service.

Air shows where planes are flown and displayed are among the most-attended sporting events in the world. During 2003 record numbers of spectators attended celebrations around the world honoring the one hundreth anniversary of the Wright brothers' first flight of the *Flyer*. The airplane's impact on the world in its first hundred years cannot be measured. Its impact on the world in the next hundred years can only be imagined.

CHAPTER SIX

Flying Into the Future

From the first flight in 1903 to 1916, the Wright brothers made nineteen different plane models. Their improvements seem minor compared with the incredible changes airplanes have undergone since the first flight of the *Flyer*.

Power Plants and Jet Propulsion

The development of Liberty Engines in 1917 was a major step forward in the expansion of both military and civilian aircraft. The 400-horsepower engines featured interchangeable parts and were designed to be mass produced.

The radial engine, with cylinders arranged like the spokes of a wheel, became the engine of choice after World War I. The 220-horsepower Wright Whirlwind radial engine used by Charles Lindbergh on his nonstop crossing of the Atlantic Ocean from New York to Paris in 1927 demonstrated the enormous potential of the airplane beyond battlefields.

World War II created an explosion of new aircraft technology. The most radical change in aircraft came as a result of the development of the jet engine. Jet propulsion moves planes through the air without using propellers. The jet sucks air into the front of the engine and passes it into a rapidly turning turbine to heat and pressurize it. Then

Maintaining a massive jet engine requires highly skilled mechanics trained in the latest state-of-the-art technology.

WHAT IS THE SOUND BARRIER?

The sound barrier was believed to be the speed an aircraft could not exceed without breaking apart. Sound travels through the air at different speeds, depending on altitude and temperature. Shock waves build up ahead of an aircraft as it pushes through the air. This buildup of waves increases the drag and decreases the lift of an airplane's wings. An airplane without sufficient power can become uncontrollable.

The flight of the Bell X-1 rocket plane (below) on October 14, 1947, by test pilot Chuck Yeager proved that an aircraft with sufficient power could safely break through the wall of shock waves into smooth flight. The X-1 became the first airplane to fly faster than the speed of sound when Yeager flew 700 miles (1,126 km) per hour at 43,000 feet (13,106 m) above sea level.

the air is forced out the rear of the engine, providing the enormous thrust that propels an airplane forward.

When World War II began, France, Germany, Great Britain, and Italy were the leading air powers. The United States was fifth. During the six years of the war, the United States became the air power leader, producing more than 100,000 bombers, fighters, trainers, and transports. The technology developed during the war continued to be applied in commercial aircraft construction.

The jet engine appeared near the beginning of World War II on German aircraft. With the technology of the jet engine, the airplane moved the world into a new era known as "the jet age." British Overseas Airways Corporation had the first commercial jetliner service.

Today the jet engine is used in all combat aircraft and for most civilian transport. However, the jet engine is not practical or technologically suitable for use on most small aircraft.

Rapid Changes

Slower biplanes were replaced by faster monoplanes with only one pair of wings. All-metal construction replaced fabric-covered wood frames. Better airport facilities and air traffic control systems were required to support advanced aircraft designs.

The air traffic control system is a vast network of people and equipment that ensures the safe operation of all

Experienced air traffic controllers at Chicago's O'Hare International Airport provide pilots with information needed for safe arrivals and departures.

commercial and private aircraft. The pilot is responsible for the safe operation of the aircraft, while an air traffic controller is responsible for coordinating the movement of air traffic within certain airspace.

Transcontinental commercial air service between New York and Los Angeles began on October 25, 1930. The most spectacular advances in aircraft operations began

This crowd of people, gathered at the unveiling of the Boeing 777 in 1994, would all fit inside *the jumbo jet.*

with successful commercial passenger jet service in the 1950s. The Boeing 707, flown by Pan American Airways, began carrying passengers across the Atlantic Ocean in 1958. The 707 was followed by the first jumbo jet, the Boeing 747. The 747 carries more than four hundred passengers. Now such airliners as the Boeing 777 routinely fly nonstop from New York to Paris and London. They travel at more than 500 miles (805 km) per hour. Students can visit a museum in Paris on Friday and be back home in the United States in time for school on Monday.

THE SR-71 BLACKBIRD

The SR-71 Blackbird is the fastest air-breathing jet in the world. It can maintain a speed of around 2,000 miles (3,218 km) per hour. It is used as an unarmed spy plane for taking photos from 85,000 feet (25,908 m) above the earth. The aerial photography equipment aboard the SR-71 can produce a clear picture of a golf ball on a golf course taken from 80,000 feet (24,384 m) above the earth.

Navigating the Infinite Highways of the Air

There were no navigation instruments in the first airplanes to help pilots know how to get where they were going. A compass was the only piece of navigation equipment the pilot could rely on. At first, people would build bonfires at a prearranged time along a certain route. The pilot would find the way by flying from bonfire to bonfire.

Light beacons were then established. Pilots could fly from one light beacon to the next if there was sufficient visibility. The need to fly when visibility was limited brought about the use of radio beams for navigation. By setting the frequency of a radio beam on the receiver in the airplane, the pilot could navigate between two points. Radio-beam navigation enabled pilots to fly without seeing the ground below. This made the airplane a safer, more efficient means of transportation.

More modern radar navigation systems, developed during the last decade of the twentieth century, are now being replaced by the Global Positioning System. The GPS is a system of twenty-four satellites orbiting more than 12,500 miles (20,113 km) above the earth. Each satellite broadcasts a precise data signal received by a GPS receiver in the airplane. The receiver can immediately determine the airplane's position, altitude, speed, and direction anywhere in the world, regardless of the weather.

Pilots today can choose to use precise navigational information available from satellites orbiting the earth like the Galileo navigation system.

GPS technology is being used to operate unmanned aircraft known as drones. These airplanes are rapidly being developed for military use and to meet a variety of humanitarian needs.

The Supersonic Transport

The *Concorde* is known as a supersonic transport because it flew faster than the speed of sound. It made its first commercial flight on January 21, 1976. This was not quite seven years after astronaut Neil Armstrong became the first human to walk on the moon.

The Concorde *super sonic transport with its delta wings and needle-sharp nose was unmistakable anywhere it landed.*

The *Concorde*'s cruising speed was 1,336 miles (2,150 km) per hour at an altitude of 55,000 feet (16,764 m). It could travel from Paris or London to the East Coast of the United States in three and a half hours. Commercial flights of the supersonic *Concorde* ended in 2003 because of the extremely high costs of operating the aircraft.

The Space Shuttle and Beyond

The space shuttles are winged, aircraftlike orbiters. They are launched with a large rocket booster, and they land like an airplane. The first space shuttle flew in 1981.

A shuttle travels 5 miles (8 km) per second as it orbits the earth. In twelve seconds—the length of time of Orville Wright's first flight at Kitty Hawk—the shuttle travels 60 miles (97 km)!

Research is under way for a new generation of aircraft beyond the space shuttle. These hypersonic airplanes are being designed to fly more than five times the speed of sound, using engines with no moving parts. A passenger aboard a hypersonic airplane may be able to fly from Kitty Hawk, North Carolina, to Los Angeles, California, in less than an hour.

Johnny Moore could hardly believe what he saw when he witnessed the Wright *Flyer* lift off the ground. It is even harder for us to imagine what awaits us as we continue flying into the future.

The space shuttle Endeavor *returns to the Mojave Desert in California after a successful docking with the International Space Station.*

The Airplane: A Timeline

1894 — Octave Chanute's book, *Progress in Flying Machines*, is published. *p. 30*

1900 — Wright glider experiments begin at Kitty Hawk, North Carolina. *p. 37*

1903 — The Wright brothers file for their first patent based on their 1902 glider. *p. 44*

Orville Wright pilots the first sustained flight of a manned, powered, heavier-than-air machine at Kitty Hawk. *p. 12*

1906 — First patent is issued to the Wright brothers by the U.S. government. *p. 46*

1912 — Wilbur Wright dies of typhoid fever. *p. 46*

1918 — The United States officially establishes airmail service. *p. 50*

1927 — Charles Lindbergh flies nonstop solo across the Atlantic. *p. 59*

1930 — Transcontinental commercial air service between New York and Los Angeles begins. *p. 63*

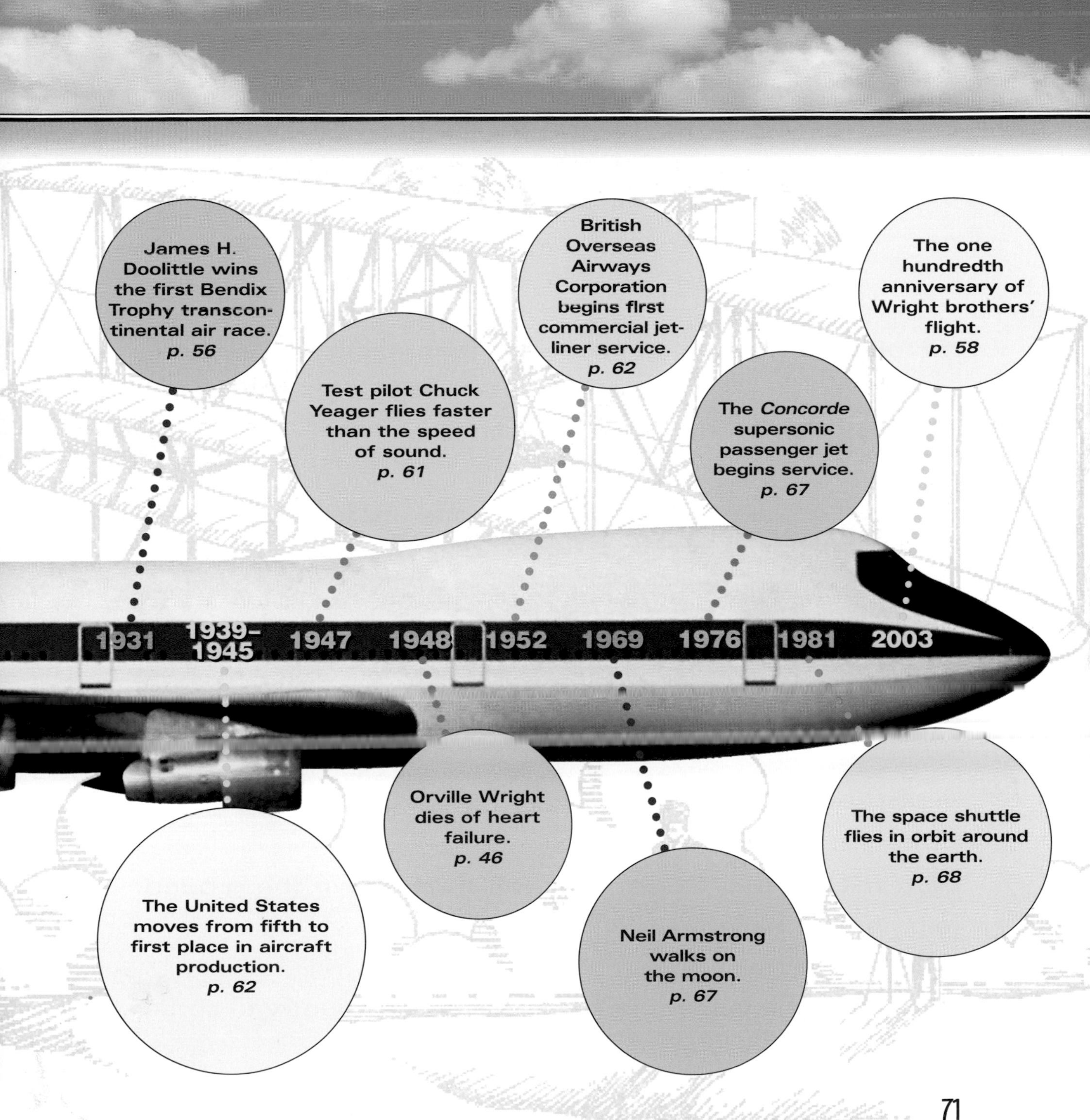
James H. Doolittle wins the first Bendix Trophy transcontinental air race. p. 56
1931
The United States moves from fifth to first place in aircraft production. p. 62
1939–1945
Test pilot Chuck Yeager flies faster than the speed of sound. p. 61
1947
Orville Wright dies of heart failure. p. 46
1948
British Overseas Airways Corporation begins first commercial jetliner service. p. 62
1952
Neil Armstrong walks on the moon. p. 67
1969
The Concorde supersonic passenger jet begins service. p. 67
1976
The space shuttle flies in orbit around the earth. p. 68
1981
The one hundredth anniversary of Wright brothers' flight. p. 58
2003

Glossary

airfoil: A surface such as a wing that reacts to the wind

airways: Paths traveled by airplanes

biplane: A plane with two wings, one above the other

glider: A heavier-than-air aircraft without an engine

heavier-than-air: Object that will fall to the ground when not in motion

isolation: Being separated from others by distance

lighter-than-air: Object that will float above the ground (e.g., hot-air balloon)

migration: Movement of people from one country to settle in another country

Outer Banks: A chain of narrow, sandy islands along the coast of North Carolina

patent: A legal document protecting ownership

perishable: Likely to spoil or decay

piston: Part of a combustion engine that produces power when it moves

propeller: A blade that is actually a vertical wing; when turned by an engine, it pulls or pushes an airplane through the air

rudders: Flat, movable airfoils that control direction, left or right

transcontinental: Crossing an entire continent

To Find Out More

Books and Photographs

Berliner, Don. *Before the Wright Brothers*: Mankato, MN: Lerner Publications Company, 1990.

Schulz, Walter A. *Will and Orv*. Minneapolis: Carolrhoda Books, 1992.

Wright, Wilbur. *Photographs by the Wright Brothers*. A micropublication of prints from the glass negatives in the Library of Congress, Washington, D.C., published in 1978 to commemorate the seventy-fifty anniversary of flight.

Yolen, Jane. *My Brothers' Flying Machine: Wilbur, Orville, and Me*. New York: Little, Brown & Company, 2003.

Web Sites

The Franklin Institute

http://sln.fi.edu/

This site contains lots of information about the Wright brothers and their experiments.

Smithsonian National Air and Space Museum
http://www.nasm.si.edu/
This museum is designated by the U.S. Congress to collect, preserve, and display the history of flight.

United States Air Force Museum
http://www.wpafb.af.mil/museum/index.htm
This is the Web site of the world's oldest aviation museum.

The Wright Brothers Airplane Company
http://www.first-to-fly.com
This virtual museum features online exhibits of the Wright Brothers Aeroplane Company and the Museum of Pioneer Aviation.

Video

Kitty Hawk: The Wright Brothers' Journey of Invention. David Garrigus Video & Film Productions, Waco, TX (2003).

Wilbur & Orville Wright: Dreams of Flying. Claypoint Productions in association with A&E Television Networks, New York (1994).

Organizations

There are more than 1,500 aviation-related organizations around the world, each focusing on particular areas of interest related to aircraft and flying. Here are three of the most respected in the industry that offer memberships, educational opportunities, and activities at the student level.

Aircraft Owners and Pilots Association (AOPA)
421 Aviation Way
Frederick, Maryland 21701-4798
http://www.aopa.org/

Experimental Aircraft Association (EAA)
PO Box 3086
Oshkosh, Wisconsin 54903-3086
http://www.eaa.org

Civil Air Patrol (CAP)
105 South Hansell Street
Building 714
Maxwell Air Force Base, Alabama 36112-6332
http://www.capnhq.gov

Index

Page numbers in *italics* indicate illustrations

About the Author

Nancy Robinson Masters has been writing about people and planes for more than twenty years. She is the author of sixteen books. As a freelance writer and licensed pilot, Nancy has traveled the world, serving a variety of humanitarian programs. "The most important thing I do in life is presenting visiting-author programs in schools," Nancy says. "I want kids to understand they can achieve their dreams through the power of reading and writing."

Nancy also presents staff development workshops for teachers and motivational programs for business and civic groups.

Nancy grew up on a cotton farm in West Texas. She lives near Abilene, Texas with her husband, veteran aviator Bill Masters. They have four dogs and four cats and are actively involved in restoring and flying antique aircraft.